A Celebration of Humanity

GORDON BOSTIC

Primix Publishing
East Brunswick Office Evolution
1 Tower Center Boulevard, Ste 1510
East Brunswick, NJ 08816
www.primixpublishing.com
Phone: 1-800-538-5788

Published by Primix Publishing: 10/16/2024

ISBN: 979-8-88703-410-2(sc)
ISBN: 979-8-88703-411-9(e)

Library of Congress Control Number: 2024917430

PR MIX
PUBLISHING
THE WRITE CHOICE

Contents

❦

Acceptance

It is acceptance that we seek
In all we do and say.
Rejection is our greatest fear
Where we are pushed away.

For all we want is to belong
And not be left outside.
For we are social animals
And from that cannot hide.

And anything that challenges
Our efforts to belong
Becomes to us an obstacle
Acceptance to prolong.

So, when acceptance is denied
We're left with no recourse
But to stare in from the outside
And beg until we're hoarse.

The Beast

They considered him a monster
Due to deformity.
For he'd been born with horns and tail
As Satan's thought to be.

They made his life a living hell
Not caring in the least
As the name they had given him
Had been the filthy beast.

So, as a child, he had been shunned
With no friends to be made.
His life was worse than miserable
As he, they would degrade.

But, finally, he came of age
And quickly disappeared.
Though no one in his neighborhood
Did anything but cheered.

Grace the Bearded Lady

Her mother called her beautiful
Though most would disagree.
For she was born with facial hair
A grown man would envy.

And she'd been humiliated
When people laughed and stared.
She was the butt of many jokes
Though feigned, she had not cared.

But inside it was killing her
For nothing that she did
Had removed all the facial hair
She wished to have been rid.

So, she was just an oddity
Most people had ignored.
Except for the occasion when
The outside she explored.

No Charity

For some, there is no charity
Society bestows.
The ones outside of commonplace
Despite how great their woes.

The ones the world would gladly shun
And turn their backs upon.
Because of singularities
Genetics had passed on.

The ones they deemed were merely freaks
Who were devoid of souls.
Those punished by the hand of God
For lacking His controls.

For those, there is no charity
Just ridicule and scorn.
Because they had been different
In how they had been born.

The Bearer of the Light

He was the bearer of the light
As all were drawn to him.
For he exuded confidence
That filled him to the brim.

He was a dreamer who dreamed dreams
That no one dreamed before.
And he had been so resolute
In what his dreams stood for.

He had a mythic quality
To cajole and persuade
That all believed his promises
Though few he really made.

He was the bearer of the light
In which they wished to shine.
For it's his dream that they dreamed too
Believing it divine.

Nothing Ordinary

He had a dream he dared pursue
In celebrating man.
It was a show that he decided
Imagination ran.

Though people won't admit to it
They're drawn to the bizarre.
So, his show would present to them
Real people as they are.

And also acts of derring-do
Providing them a thrill.
Surely nothing ordinary
For which they would sit still.

But he needed special people
That he'd train to perform.
Although no one ordinary
Would fit on his platform.

Collecting Human Oddities

He roamed the earth in search of those
He needed for his show.
And charmed them into joining him
To give his dream a go.

The first he found were Sam and Dan
And gladly they had joined.
The twins were total opposites
Although were born conjoined.

Then he found Ivan the Dog Boy,
Who was covered in fur.
And then Mei Ling with her tattoos
That covered all of her.

He then discovered Gregory
Who's nearly eight feet tall.
And paired him up with Nickolas
Who was but three feet small.

In Jacque, he found a heavy man
With weight measured in stones.
Then next, he found the polish girl
Who seemed to have no bones.

Most of them human oddities
Their mothers disavowed.
The outcasts of society
Who stood out from the crowd.

Not judged by what their hearts contain
But on their strange physiques.
And people turned away from them
Believing they were freaks.

But he'd something to offer them
That they had not known before.
A place where they're accepted with
Dignity to restore.

Though most believed it was a dream
There're some who were unsure.
For it's hard to trust anyone
Whose motives were obscure.

A List of Candidates

He had a list of candidates
From which he had to choose.
Performers who'd reached out to him
Believing in his views.

She was the queen of the trapeze
Who had no sense of fear.
And though she had been gorgeous too
She'd let no one get near.

He'd heard Kris was the very best
But she had problems too.
They said she suffered socially
And had no friends they knew.

She was most happy in the air
Where she was truly free.
Where no one could get close to her
And it was only she.

Jean Pierre had been world renown
For walking the high wires.
But he was very arrogant
And slave to his desires.

The polish girl had been quite shy
And would not give her name.
But she was like a rubber band
Which was her claim to fame.

Together they're the centerpiece
He'd build his show upon.
Adding those plucked from the shadows
To which crowds would be drawn.

For due to curiosity
Of what appears bizarre
He thought the show would be a hit
And each of them a star.

Gordon Bostic

The Union

The union bosses came to him
When hearing of the show.
They had the work force he required
Which was the way to go.

But there were things they must demand
Or there could be no deal.
He cautiously had asked them what
Though feared what they'd reveal.

But their demands he found insane
And calmly told them so.
For he would find another way
To bring about his show.

Their anger they could not contain
As it shone from their eyes.
He knew he'd made an enemy
Which likely was unwise.

A Little Good

It was a time of great despair
With many unemployed.
So, he would hire day laborers
And 'round the show deployed.

But there were many more of them
Than he could ever use.
So, he faced the predicament
Having to pick and choose.

But that had led to jealousy
And some disgruntlement
From all of those he never chose
But felt entitlement.

And though he thought he knew their pain
He did the best he could
To spread around what wealth he had
And do a little good.

He knew ill feelings may exist
From those he could not aid.
But prayed that they would understand
That choices must be made.

Gordon Bostic

The Tent

He purchased a gigantic tent
In which to host the show.
Then hired a bunch of laborers
To help to make it grow.

The tent had been a massive thing
It took two days to raise.
And then the rigging was installed
To dazzle and amaze.

Then finally they put in place
Large blocks that formed three rings.
Which would grow to be the symbol
Of joy the circus brings.

Once the tent had been erected
Trailers were put in place
As housing for the performers
And their own private space.

For most that was a luxury
That they had never known.
Because of their appearances
The streets they had been shown.

But now there was community
And they had found a home
Next to the huge monstrosity
They called the canvass dome.

First Day

On the first day of their training
There's nothing that went well.
The twins would not stop bickering
And all else went to hell.

As a gathering of strangers
Not knowing who to trust.
For they'd all faced life as loners
And now forced to adjust.

Immediately, Jean Pierre
Became the problem child.
As he proclaimed himself the star
Which drove the others wild.

The polish girl had disappeared
Disturbed by the turmoil.
And Kris began to lose her cool
With blood about to boil.

Then finger pointing grew intense
As who it was to blame.
Though most would vote for Jean Pierre
There's fault they all could claim.

He sadly watched it all unfold
And his dreams disappear.
He'd hoped they'd be a family
But they were nowhere near.

Gordon Bostic

Then Grace stood up and said to them,
"If we don't get this right.
We'll never have a chance of home
But return to our plight."

The polish girl then reappeared
And took Grace by the hand.
The others seemed to settle down
As though it had been planned.

And they began to train again
With a new attitude.
Perhaps his dream was still alive
As joy they did exude.

No Such Thing as Paradise

There's no such thing as paradise
When people are involved.
Because of petty jealousies
That seem to have evolved.

Though most accepted what they had
There always are a few
Who don't believe there's justice done
In what they think they're due.

There're always personalities
That seem to just conflict.
As they can never get along
But seek pain to inflict.

And so, the same was true with them.
There're some who had to go.
For their attitudes interfered
With what he wished to show.

Gordon Bostic

The Clowns

He went and hired a group of clowns
Who promised to amuse.
But all of them seemed devious
And too in love with booze.

The training they're required to do
They simply would ignore.
For half the time, they were too drunk
To stand upon the floor.

And twice they were caught rummaging
Through things that weren't their own.
Though harshly he'd come down on them
No changes had been shown.

That's when he came to recognize
The clowns they must be rid.
They were merely a distraction
Through bad things that they did.

Bryce

Bryce was one of the laborers
Who worked behind the scene.
He seemed to be responsible
And his work was pristine.

But Bryce had shown initiative
The others had not shown.
So, he offered full employment
Only to Bryce alone.

He was in charge of laborers
And technical aspect.
He ran the things behind the scenes
Knowing what they'd expect.

Bryce was enamored with the show
And all who did perform.
He thought the show spectacular
And was outside the norm.

Whenever he could find the chance
He'd slyly watch them train.
He wished he was a part of it
If skills he could attain.

He thought they all were marvelous
But Kris, especially.
He watched her soar above the ground
And fly majestically.

He thought if there's a place for him
It was on the trapeze.
If he could summon the courage
And Kris, he could appease.

The Dream Explained

On the first night, they had gathered
To hear his dream explained.
For all had been quite curious
What thoughts he entertained.

His dream had been to have a show
That featured all of them.
A show where ev'ryone could see
They're the crème de la crème.

A show to prove they're no diff'rent
Than any in the crowd.
And even with their appearance
They also could be proud.

What he saw a celebration
Of all humanity.
Where those with diff'rent shapes and forms
Were one community.

Despite religion, race, or creed
They all together stood.
As close as any family
In what they had withstood.

And all committed to the show
In which they would perform.
Where they could truly be themselves
With no need to conform.

Then afterward they had mingled
And sat down to a feast.
That's when he introduced them to
The one known as the Beast.

Bad Attitude

Ev'ry night they'd dine together
Though Kris would eat alone.
The others found her standoffish
And left her on her own.

Then one night, Grace sat next to her
And asked if she's all right.
But Kris, at first just stared at her
As if she's impolite.

Grace told her if she'd like to talk
She's a good listener.
But Kris had simply stared at her
As though a prisoner.

Then Grace got up and walked away
Giving Kris solitude.
The others gave Kris a wide berth
Due to her attitude.

From Across the Room

Bryce saw her from across the room
And to her had been drawn.
He thought she was as beautiful
As was a perfect dawn.

But Kris was not that talkative
Although Bryce truly tried.
She barely spoke to anyone,
In fact, she seemed to hide.

She found a corner where she stood
Away from ev'ryone.
So, while all the others mingled,
Kris chose to meet no one.

Her mother made her daughter strong
And that was by design.
Her mother taught her not to trust
'Cause trust was not benign.

For there are penalties with trust
Her mother harshly paid.
When finding by the one she loved
Was selfishly betrayed.

The Training

They trained and trained for weeks on end
Preparing for the show.
For there was choreography
And moves they had to know.

With so much to coordinate,
The training was intense.
Though ev'ry time there was a break,
Bryce tried breach her defense.

Usually, Kris turned away
But one day turned to him
And asked him what his problem was
That he'd risk life and limb.

He said that he'd called out to her
Because he wished to learn.
He hoped that she would tutor him
To do what he'd most yearn.

Then she paused in hesitation
But did not turn around.
As though she gave some thought to it,
But answer had not found.

The Only You That You Can Be

The only you that you can be
Is who you really are.
You can assume identities
But they won't take you far.

We can deny who we may be
Because we are ashamed.
But deep inside we have to know
This is the life we've claimed.

We can pretend we're someone else
But that's only pretend.
There's nothing good that comes from it
That helps us in the end.

The only person we can be
Is the one we were made.
And till we come to grips with that,
Achievements are waylaid.

He Made Her Smile

He stood upon the small platform
With courage to acquire.
It seemed to be a long way down
Which caused him to perspire.

He grabbed the trapeze and swung out
Then quickly lost his grip.
He hit the netting pretty hard
And feared he broke a hip.

He struggled free from the netting
And climbed back up again
To stand upon the small platform
And give it one more spin.

Kris came to her morning training
And found Bryce in the air.
Thank God a net had been employed
As mostly he'd end there.

She must admit she was amused
To see him try and fail.
But he proved to be no quitter
Despite how much he fell.

She thought about approaching him,
Then thought she'd wait awhile.
She can't recall how long it's been
Since she was made to smile.

Gordon Bostic

The Picket Lines

The stories of the show had spread
To places far and wide.
There were requests for them to tour
Across the countryside.

It seemed the show was in demand
Most ev'rywhere but here.
Where most performers were afraid
The outside to go near.

The picket lines had posed a threat
That very much was real.
For in their chants were hateful things
They chose to not conceal.

And the hostility had grown
With ev'ry passing day.
Though nothing that he offered them
Would make them go away.

The Choreographer

To Mike, they were a motley crew
Of freak and vagabond.
But he delivered best he could,
And they had gone beyond.

Although at first he had been shocked
When he had met his class.
As people, they had grown on him,
And shock was soon to pass.

His admiration, they had won
Because they worked so hard
And he had grown quite fond of them
In learning his dance card.

But this time, it would be for real,
And he can't interfere.
He only prayed it all went well,
For they deserved a cheer.

Preparations

They nervously prepared themselves
For their first matinée.
They knew how hard they worked for this
And hoped that work would pay.

What if the crowd did not embrace
The essence of the show?
What if the crowd should turn on them?
They'd nowhere else to go.

He stood before them so composed
It seemed to calm them down.
As he exuded confidence
In which he wished they'd drown.

He told them they were underdogs.
Most came to see them fail.
But there's an option left to them
That still was theirs to tell.

For their show's a celebration
Of who they truly are.
They could have sunk into despair
Instead, they've come so far.

The Matinée

The tent had been completely dark
When the spotlight came on
To show Kris soaring near the top
Whom all eyes were upon.

Then as the lights began to rise
They started to parade.
As girls on ropes were hoisted up
In aerial cascade.

The audience was mesmerized
By ev'rything they saw.
The applause had been thunderous
As most were wrapped in awe.

Then as the show came to its end,
The audience had stood
While they roared with their approval
Of what they thought was good.

Gordon Bostic

The Walk

Bryce looked and saw that it was late
But found he could not sleep.
He still was pumped up from the show
And rest would have to keep.

He then decided take a walk
To try and clear his head.
That's when he found Kris by the tent
Just staring straight ahead.

He asked her if she was all right.
She said she was okay.
She found she could not fall asleep
Nor wind down from the day.

He said that he'd been sleepless too
And thought he'd take a walk.
Perhaps she'd like to walk with him
And maybe they could talk.

They shared some small talk as they walked
But nothing personal.
She revealed a sense of humor
When caught as casual.

Then when she said that she was tired
He walked her to her place.
He told her he enjoyed the walk
And a smile lit her face.

The Critics

The critics had been critical
Of ev'rything they saw.
They found no value in the show
And surely weren't in awe.

They called the show a novelty
That was not worth the price.
Unfit for high society
Had been their best advice.

And they claimed it was a circus
With no redeeming grace
Just a respite for the masses
Who'd nothing else to taste.

An affront to the theater
Where allegiance would lie.
They critically predicted
They'd wait for it to die

No Promises

The next day, Bryce was there again
And showed the same success.
The net became his new best friend
For he was just a mess.

But he showed he was persistent
That much, she must admit.
Though the limits of his knowledge
Was only half of it.

The next day, as if right on queue
Kris found him there again.
But feared that he would kill himself
If she did not step in.

So, she began to work with him
And show him all the ropes.
But offered him no promises
Nor fostered any hopes.

The Outcome of the Show

The show had been a huge success
And word began to spread.
The critics had not damaged it
Instead, its fame, they fed.

The show was growing in its fame
With tickets in demand.
And ev'ry night the crowds poured in
To fill the huge grandstand.

And ev'ry night, the show improved
As they grew more at ease.
They found they were receptive to
A crowd they wished to please.

But he was always tinkering
And adding to the show.
He found quintuplets who breathed fire
And could not let them go.

Perhaps exotic animals
Would add to their appeal.
For people would be curious
To see that they were real.

And if the animals performed,
They would enrich the show.
So, he began a global search
To see if this was so.

Gordon Bostic

The Animals

The animals enhanced the show
With all that they could do.
Before the show, they were displayed
As though it was a zoo.

They took great care maintaining them
And making sure they're well.
For they were now part of the show
And here they'd come to dwell.

From elephants to the large cats,
The people loved them all.
And the animals had seemed pleased
The people they'd enthrall.

Society Looked Down on Them

Society looked down on them
As though they had no worth.
For all of them were commoners
As proven by their birth.

They were the dregs of humankind
Who should be locked away.
Instead, they were celebrated
As special in some way.

Society was horrified
They from the shadows sprang.
Those misfits of society
Who looked more like a gang.

Society looked down on them
With contempt and disdain.
As they'd parade beneath their tent
As normal they would feign.

Gordon Bostie

Once They Saw Him Smile

Though the Beast had a gentle heart
His looks seemed to conceal.
He was a mainstay of the show
With some bizarre appeal.

Most children we're afraid of him
Until they saw him smile.
For then his face would simply beam,
And he'd not seemed that vile.

The children in their innocence
Would ask him what's his name.
For Beast seemed inappropriate
And one he should disclaim.

And ev'ry time he'd smile and say
His true real name was Guy.
For Beast was just a moniker
Kids teased to make him cry.

The Ambassador

The polish girl was very shy
And could not handle stress.
Her talent was phenomenal
But, otherwise, a mess.

But little children, she adored
So, before ev'ry show,
She'd occupy the main entrance
And tell them all hello.

In some ways, an ambassador
Secure in her good will.
The polish girl was insecure
But kids gave her a thrill.

Gordon Bostic

The Activists

Some activists became enraged
He acquired animals.
For this was not their habitat
And maybe their downfalls.

They filed petitions with the court
Claiming they were abused.
The animals had certain rights
And they weren't being used.

The judge, however, disagreed
And threw the whole thing out.
The activists though were not done
Leaving nothing to doubt.

And so, they joined the picket lines
As they would protest too.
The union now they sided with
Though with a diff'rent view.

The Passion

The passion that he felt for her
He knew he had to hide.
She did not seem the loving type
Though she'd taught him to glide.

There was a certain strength in her
He secretly admired.
For she was driven to succeed
More than should be desired.

If she possessed a softer side
It's one he'd never seen.
But there was something underneath
That she would deeply screen.

He knew it was not logical,
And he could not explain.
The passion that he felt for her
He knew he must contain.

Gordon Bostic

On Tour

From time to time, they'd go on tour
And do some shows for free.
For he believed in joy for all
And acts of charity.

The orphanage had been one place
Where they had loved to go.
For the kids got so excited
When they would see the show.

The trapeze, they could not transport
So, they used special bars.
Though Bryce was not adept with them
While Kris could touch the stars.

So, while Kris drew the oohs and aahs
And wonder of them all.
Poor Bryce had made the children laugh
As he would slip and fall.

Then when the show had reached its end,
The children, they would meet.
And they would interface with them
To make the day complete.

The Invitation

The president invited them
To see the capitol.
For he'd heard stories of the show
And wished to see it all.

He was amazed at what he saw
In these strange oddities.
But he found that they were gifted
And were eager to please.

Though he found the show refreshing
He said he was concerned.
Since they were human oddities
Could people's hearts be turned?

He replied to the president
They wished to celebrate
Not the depth of the diff'rences
But sameness they create.

Dark Alternatives

The union leaders were upset
Their people were not used.
They claimed his workers were unskilled
And often were abused.

The threats they made were very veiled
And dark in their intent.
They were not happy with the shows
Lack of their involvement.

They warned of dark alternatives
Should demands not be met.
The circus could be dangerous
Despite its safety net.

He viewed the threats as serious
So, they must be on guard.
They spoke of dark alternatives
Which he feared could be hard.

Seeds of Distrust

There was a string of accidents
That briefly cursed the show
With evidence of tampering
As if they're meant to know

It was a message clearly sent,
And threat that was received.
For someone was unhappy with
The things that they'd achieved.

Though no one had been put at risk,
And no one had been harmed.
There was a sense of urgency,
And all had been alarmed.

They were unsure of whom to trust
For someone's been inside.
The tampering could not be done
By one from the outside.

So now they all were placed at odds
Not knowing whom to trust.
And the show was clearly damaged
By the seeds of distrust.

The Touch

By accident, Bryce touched her hand
Yet, she'd not pulled away.
So, he had let it linger there
Chancing what Kris may say.

But Kris did not say anything
Which caught him by surprise.
And so, he dared to look at her
And stared into her eyes.

There was no need to speak a word.
Her eyes said that she knew.
And the feeling was mutual
As she cared for him too.

The Message That Was Sent

They all had hated Jean Pierre
Because he was a bore.
He claimed he was a superstar
Which all grew to abhor.

But when the accident occurred
They all had been surprised.
For no one wished to see him die
Although he was despised.

The safety netting had collapsed
So, he went straight to ground.
The crowd was shocked and horrified
When they had heard the sound.

Police came to investigate
And ruled an accident.
But Bryce thought it was more likely
It was a message sent.

For when the netting was repaired,
Some hardware was missing.
And there was no explanation
Which led to questioning.

A Simple Strategy

The union leaders were annoyed
Their people were not used.
Instead, he hired day laborers
And they were not amused.

And their displeasure they had shown
By picketing the show.
They tried to keep the people out
With taunts, they should not go.

Then the performers they'd harass
And goad them into fights.
For performers who were injured
Can't perform under lights.

It was a simple strategy
Designed to kill the show.
For the union proved vindictive
In how far it would go.

True Strength

True strength grows through adversity
And they had seen their share.
From accidents to sabotage
It made them well aware.

For there were forces hard at work
Intent to see them fail.
Who'd it seemed would stop at nothing
To make their lives a hell.

"If you see yourselves as victims
That's all you'll ever be.
And you will never rise above
The limits that you see."

"So, it's a choice that must be made
To go forth or give in
For there's no glory to achieve
If outside forces win."

Gordon Bostic

The Charlatan

They thought he was a charlatan
And truly was lowbrow.
His appeal was from the masses
Whom they would disavow.

They thought he wished to be of them
But had no pedigree.
For it's mainly via birthright
You gained society.

His show was mainly for the dolts
Who'd be hoodwinked and fooled.
It had no class nor dignity
Unless it was retooled.

And people of that caliber
Were well beneath their gaze.
For those in high society
Would never offer praise.

But those in high society
Had missed it by a mile.
There can be no greater calling
Than making people smile.

Her Respect He Earned

He listened to her ev'ry word
And did as he was told.
She was the mistress of the air,
And he not yet that bold.

He watched her soar above the rings
So, fluid in her grace.
That's where she was the happiest
With no concerns to face.

She was so agile in the air
As though she once had wings.
And he was just a novice who
Had never mastered swings.

But now he found he's in her debt
Because she dared to try
To help him be a part of this
Though he did not know why.

She had admired how hard he worked
And how quickly he learned.
She saw potential lived in him
And her respect, he earned.

At dinner, she caused quite a stir
For she had not thought twice.
She got her food then crossed the room
And sat down next to Bryce.

A Little Honesty

Kris went to Bryce after the show
And said they'd need to talk.
He saw the panic in her eyes
And said that they should walk.

And in their silence, they had strolled
Until they were alone.
And then he turned and looked at her
With concern cold as stone.

Kris told Bryce she's not worthy of
Affections he had shown.
For she possessed a sordid past
She wished she'd never known.

Then he told Kris he's not the man
Who she thought him to be.
Perhaps a little honesty
Would serve to set them free.

Her Story

In the shadows, there is darkness
And that's all she had known.
Her stepfather took liberties
When they were left alone.

When she tried to tell her mother
Her mom would not believe.
So, she was left to his designs
With what he could conceive.

But when she thought she was of age
She chose to run away.
After she clubbed the SOB
And kicked him where he'd lay.

She roamed the streets as homeless do
And lived a life in fear.
But she swore no man would touch her
Or ever get that near.

Then a gypsy clan had found her
And taught her the trapeze.
Next found this opportunity
She quickly came to seize.

A Product of Society

A product of society
To which he had been born.
And constrained by obligations
That made him feel forlorn.

One who's given expectations
He was challenged to meet
With a future that's provided
He did not wish to greet.

Someone who had been given all
But never would be free.
A man who never asked to be
Born to society.

The Magic of the Night

It was the magic of the night
That led them to embrace.
Two strangers on a stranger course
That now they chose to face.

Two lonely souls who once were lost
That now have found their way.
Two homeless people on the street
Who found a place to stay.

Two entities merged into one
With faith and trust in place.
And in the magic of the night
Would finally embrace.

Her Puckish Side

Every morning, they'd workout
Before breakfast was served.
Kris told Bryce that he had improved
But praise, she had reserved.

He tried to do a somersault
But missed it by a hair.
He thought he'd find a new trapeze
Instead, he clutched thin air.

Then from the netting, he looked up
He saw Kris was laughing.
And she was holding the trapeze
That he'd been expecting.

Bryce rolled his eyes and had to laugh.
Kris had a puckish side.
Then he looked up and yelled to her, "
That's what you would decide?"

His Night to Shine

Tonight would be his night to shine
'Cause Kris had told him so.
For he had worked so hard for this.
Tonight he'd join the show.

Although the crowd was electric
He was nervous as hell.
Then he launched out from the platform
As Kris had wished him well.

He placed his faith in his training
As he soared through the air.
The crowd below was just a blur
Who happened to be there.

And then the moment was at hand
When he her flip would catch.
And it occurred without a hitch
As both their eyes would latch.

And all the cheers they did not hear
From those who were below.
For their attention had been locked
But not upon the show.

Gordon Bostic

In the Moment

Kris ran to Bryce after the show
And said, "Let's celebrate!"
For all of it went perfectly,
And he'd been simply great.

He'd never seen her this enthused
And was somewhat surprised.
For she was like a little girl
With twinkles in her eyes.

He held her tight then kissed her hard,
And she did not resist.
It seemed as if a fairytale
Where only they exist.

And in the moment, they both knew
A lifetime laid in wait.
So, in the throes of their desires,
Neither would hesitate.

The Disappearance

The polish girl had disappeared
Which she was wont to do.
Any time that she felt pressure
She'd withdraw from their view.

But this time had seemed different
As no one had a clue.
For always she would reappear
Which this time was not true.

They had searched for her ev'rywhere
But she was not around.
The polish girl had disappeared,
And she they had not found.

He reported she was missing
To the authorities.
And then they had to sit and wait
Though all felt ill at ease.

Then he called them all together
When he received the news.
The police found the polish girl,
But she had been abused.

They said she'd been beaten and raped
And then was left for dead.
Her state of health was not that good,
And neither was her head.

Gordon Bostic

The police had found no answers,
But it seemed clear to him.
She most likely was abducted,
And that made this most grim.

Kris and Grace went to visit her,
And she did not look well.
She had been beaten half to death
Which caused her brain to swell.

The doctors held out little hope
Of full recovery.
Her injuries were most severe
Which left them both teary.

Though none were held responsible,
Both were sure that they knew
Exactly of the circumstance,
But nothing could they do.

A Pall Had Fallen over Them

A pall had fallen over them
For much they had endured.
At first, it had been Jean Pierre,
Now this event occurred.

As though the circus had been cursed
Or placed under a spell,
For something had been hard at work
That they could not dispel.

It seemed the magic had been dulled
In what they tried to do.
As though the celebration failed
As it had been doomed to.

Then he reminded one and all
That they were not at fault.
It was not something they had done
But rather an assault.

The only way their dream could die
Is if it's by their hand.
They needed to collect themselves
And choose to make a stand.

Haters Have to Hate

It seems that haters have to hate
So, target they will find.
For hatred's the uniting force
Through which they come to bind.

No reason do they clearly need
As one they will create.
For haters need to hate something
Because they live to hate.

No matter where the hate comes from
There's always some to find.
For haters have a need to hate
If only in their mind.

And now their sights were set on them
As they were under fire.
For anything that's different
Just fuels a hater's ire.

Life Had Been Too Hard on Her

Bryce searched for Kris all afternoon
Once he had heard the news.
In fear the news stirred memories
Of acts she'd not excuse.

When her abusive stepfather
Had forced himself on her.
And this would bring back memories
That she would best defer.

He found her by the willow grove
And she was just a mess.
While crying uncontrollably
She tried to him confess.

But all he did was hold her tight
And tried to reassure.
It happened to the polish girl,
But he'd keep her secure.

And to himself, he swore an oath
That she, he would protect.
For life had been too hard on her,
And that he would correct.

Was She the One?

He woke to find her lying there
Just staring straight at him.
Though her face showed signs of worry
With eyes that looked real grim.

He thought that this could not be good
But after yesterday.
He knew emotions would run high
And she'd have things to say.

Kris asked Bryce if she was the one
And if he's really sure.
She knew that she was damaged goods
And surely was not pure.

He simply turned and smiled at her,
Of that he had no doubt.
There's no one in the whole wide world
But her he thought about.

And then he told her she was wrong.
She's not damaged at all.
He was drawn to her character
And how she stood so tall.

Although it's true she's beautiful
It was her strength of will
That made him fall in love with her
And made his heart standstill.

As Though in Sympathy

The picket lines had grown less vile
As though in sympathy.
For even they had been appalled
By the brutality.

Although opinions had not changed
Not one of them approved
Of things that had been happening
Where people were removed.

The circus was their enemy
Of which they would be rid.
But not a single one of them
Approved of what some did.

The Negativity

There were no critics anymore,
For there was not the need.
The circus had been compromised,
And it was left to bleed.

The disappearance caused a stir
And left many in doubt.
What was the purpose of the show?
And what was it about?

It seemed that negativity
Was all the show had known.
For accidents were now in vogue
Though had been overblown.

And though the crowds kept pouring in
Despite each exposé
That called the circus dangerous
And should be swept away.\

Society Had Been Appalled

Society had been appalled
To see the show survived.
For they had paid off miscreants
To see the show deprived.

The warnings had been clearly sent
Though most had been ignored.
They felt the need to escalate,
And options had explored.

With no abduction authorized
They too were in the dark.
Whoever harmed the polish girl
Had not been theirs to spark.

Although they wished the circus gone,
This act had been extreme.
And they feared that the consequence
Was nothing they'd redeem.

Kris and Grace

Kris saw Grace sitting all alone
Which Kris had thought was strange.
For Grace was so gregarious,
And groups, she would arrange.

To see her sitting all alone
Was not a common sight.
So, Kris had calmly gone to her
To see if she's all right.

The polish girl had been her friend
And this had hit Grace hard.
Kris had seen that Grace was shaken
And really off her guard.

Kris told Grace she was here for her
As long as she desired.
But Kris had felt the sadness too
And comforting required.

The Show Must Go On

There had been grumblings they were jinxed.
As was the whole damn show.
Perhaps it's best they shut it down.
When he stood and said, "No!"

"There is a purpose meant for you
But up to you to find.
The only thing that's stopping you
Is purely in your mind."

"For all the limits that you know
Are by your own design.
So, you can choose to charge ahead
Or from the show resign."

And there were some who did just that
Though most would choose to stay.
The show was not the enemy
Although it looked that way.

Though some were still quite hesitant
They all agreed upon
The fact the dream was still alive
For the show must go on.

Gordon Bostic

That Night

Although with heavy hearts that night
They went out and performed.
There was a moment's silence asked
To show that they had mourned.

The crowd had tried to rally them
But it was of no use.
There was no sense of merriment,
Though that was no excuse.

The performance had been flawless,
But it was uninspired.
The image of the polish girl
Had not with them expired.

And though the crowd seemed less enthralled
Than normally they'd be.
The ovation that they received
Conveyed their sympathy.

A Closed Community

Too many accidents occurred
Because they were betrayed
By trusting people from outside
Who came inside and preyed.

They'd be their own community
And those outside they'd shun.
For trust was their commodity
Where those outside showed none.

They were berated and abused
By those from the outside.
So, they'd need to come together
With trust built from inside.

They'd be a closed community
That none outside could breach.
This way they could protect themselves
Where danger could not reach.

Gordon Bostic

Better Days

The days that followed were more calm
Than most that they had known.
Their confidence had been restored
As their performance shown.

The show continued ev'ry night
With Sunday matinees.
And every show had been sold out
As though dawned better days.

The critics had not bothered them.
In fact, left them alone.
Defections plagued the picket lines
Where gaps were clearly shown.

All thought that Bryce was good for Kris.
He pulled her from her shell.
For now, she seemed like one of them
And really fit in well.

And Sam and Dan had argued less
And seemed to get along.
But some were worried it's too calm
And something must be wrong.

A Fresh Routine

Though Kris and Bryce had talked about
Expanding their routine,
The timing never seemed quite right
Or life would intervene.

But now they seemed to have the time
Where options they'd explore.
Though Kris would simply roll her eyes
At how Bryce wished to soar.

Though she loved him with all her heart,
Sometimes she'd want to scream.
What he proposed was dangerous
More so than it would seem.

She wished to have a fresh routine
But did not wish to die.
Though ev'rything that he proposed
Would mean they'd surely try.

The New Ambassador

Grace was the new ambassador
Who welcomed one and all.
She'd occupy the main entrance
And catered to the small.

She gave directions when required
And answered questions posed.
She was lighthearted in her role
And always seemed composed.

Some asked where was the polish girl.
Grace said she's filling in.
The polish girl was very ill,
But she'd be back again.

Grace was the new ambassador
Who greeted one and all.
But mentions of the polish girl
Would make her want to bawl.

The Fire

The fire had been well underway
Before it had been seen.
And now the panic was unleashed
As smoke had formed a screen.

Confusion had enveloped them
As smoke began to build.
The crowd was their priority
As the stands had been filled.

Performers ran to help the crowd
And guide them from the flame.
Bryce tried to rally day workers
So, exits, they could frame.

But there were none that he could find
As all had disappeared.
So, he had done the best he could
To get the exits cleared.

He ordered that the animals
Should be quickly removed.
For they were in a panicked state
And needed to be moved.

The tent was like a tinderbox
That had no real defense.
And so, the fire had quickly spread
While growing more intense.

Gordon Bostie

The tent became an inferno,
But the crowd had been saved.
Though there was nothing they could do
But watch it as it caved.

Bryce came running from the tent,
But he escaped on fire.
Several quickly ran to him,
And flames, they did retire.

But Bryce was in a troubled state
And needed urgent care.
The ambulance whisked him away
With Kris reduced to prayer.

The firefighters arrived too late
To be of any use.
They were delayed by picket lines
Was what was their excuse.

The tent had been a total loss
As was most it contained.
They'd salvage anything they could
But little had remained.

He quickly took a count of heads
To see if all were there.
The numbers though did not add up
Which he was forced to share.

He then called them all together
To assess where they stood
And found Sam and Dan were missing,
And Bryce had not looked good.

They all turned to him for answers,
But none could he provide.
For he'd been shocked by what occurred
And from that could not hide.

In the debris, they found bodies,
And they had been conjoined.
There was no doubt that Sam and Dan
In death had been rejoined.

And then the tears began to flow
For all that had been lost.
The fire destroyed their one true home,
And boundaries were crossed.

The funeral was very sad
As only they were there.
No members of their family
Had seemed to even care.

Gordon Bostic

A Total Loss

The story of the tragedy
Consumed the headline news.
The circus was in disarray
When citing witness views.

The great tent was an inferno
And seemed a total loss.
The crowd was saved, a miracle
Like none they'd come across.

They asked him if he would rebuild,
But he said he's unsure.
The damage had not been assessed
So that he must defer.

There're rumors of some injuries,
But they were unconfirmed.
The fire department was on hand
Yet still the circus burned.

There were no answers to the cause
Of what had sparked the fire.
It seemed to be a total loss
As it appeared a pyre.

Recovery

When Bryce awoke he saw her there
Sitting beside the bed.
And though he tried to speak to her,
The words remained unsaid.

Kris noticed that he was awake
And kissed him on his cheek.
She told him not to try to talk
As he was still too weak.

The doctors said he would be fine,
But it would take a while.
His injuries were serious,
And then she broached a smile.

He saw the worry in her eyes
But also saw the love.
She promised to take care of him
And hovered like a dove.

She knew the truth he'd come to know,
But now was not the time.
The trapeze would be lost to him
Which he would find a crime.

But thought in his recovery,
She would not say a thing.
For hope was inspirational
And focus it can bring.

Gordon Bostic

The Aftermath

Police confirmed it was arson
And said they'd evidence.
It had been a day laborer
Who offered no defense.

He had no reason he would share
To why he set the fire.
But they suspicioned he was paid
Though did not know the buyer.

After he surveyed the damage,
He saw it was severe.
He thought there's little they could save
If they're to persevere.

With resources already thin,
He did not really know
If they could salvage just enough
To reopen the show.

Though police had called it arson,
Some lawyers disagreed
And looked to build a clientele
Like sharks in frenzy feed.

Who then followed up with law suits
In claiming negligence.
As the show was responsible.
Which to him made no sense.

But the courts seemed to entertain
Each suit as it was filed.
And the money each demanded,
Common sense had deviled.

Though this revived the activists
Who filed suits of their own.
That would remove the animals
From abuse they were shown.

Society Misunderstood

Society misunderstood
The message of the show.
They saw it as a carnival
For little did they know.

They found it a monstrosity
With no redeeming traits.
An exploitation of the poor
To satisfy its gates.

They thought themselves superior
To what it had displayed.
That merely used unfortunates
It claimed were equal made.

Society misunderstood
The nature of the show.
For it was a celebration
Where anyone could go.

Good Intentions

It was only good intentions
That set him on this course.
With a message, he felt needed
In matter of discourse.

To show that we are all the same
Despite how we appear.
For we are equal in this life
Who share in hope and fear.

There is but one humanity
That we should celebrate,
And though we've diff'rent shapes and size,
We should appreciate.

Though each of us may be unique
It's similarities
That's meant to be the bond that binds
And through which love carries

But now the outcome that they faced
Was one that's undeserved.
As the example that they've set
Should be the one preserved.

From the Shadows

He had pulled them from the shadows
But to those they'd return.
He knew the show could not survive
With suits at ev'ry turn.

What funds were left, he had replaced
Essentials for the show.
Together with the things they saved
They'd give it one last go.

The circus had been all they knew
And home it came to be.
Where a collective of strangers
Became a family.

Meanwhile the show had to go on
If only one last time.
For it appeared that it was doomed
Which they believed a crime.

He Felt Resentment Grow in Him

His heart had turned as cold as stone
When he received the news.
He found he hated all of them
And felt he had been used.

The doctors said he'd fly no more
As damage was severe.
He felt resentment grow in him
Or maybe it was fear.

Kris tried her best to comfort him,
But he pushed her away.
The trapeze now was lost to him
And so would she one day.

He should have let the people die.
What good were they to him?
If he'd looked out for number one
What lurked may look less grim.

Though Kris was told what to expect
It still was hard to deal
With one she loved so very much
Whose pain he can't conceal.

A Lack of Miracles

There're no such things as miracles
If what they feared was true.
The show would face a bitter end
With nothing they could do.

Through all the troubles they had faced,
They found ways to survive.
But now not even miracles
Could keep the show alive.

The lawsuits just kept mounting up.
More than he could defend.
The lawyers had been parasites
That broke him in the end.

There was no mercy that was shown.
No reasoning applied.
Courts simply took them at their word,
And thus, the circus died.

He claimed that he had financing,
But he would need some time.
The courts denied his one request
And took his last damn dime.

With all the debt that he incurred
From suits that had been won,
There's no amount of miracles
That he could count upon.

The Magic Man

They thought he was the magic man
As he always came through.
Whatever looked impossible
Was what he seemed to do.

And now his magic was required
If they're to save the show.
For ev'rything had been destroyed
And morale's running low.

In fact, they'd need a miracle
If there's one to be found.
For ev'rything that they held dear,
Had been burned to the ground.

So, all turned to the magic man
And prayed he knew a spell.
For otherwise the show was done
Without a fond farewell.

His Dreams

There were no dreams that he had dreamed
That were not dreams of her.
For ev'rything about the girl
Had caused his heart to stir.

She was the magic in the night
That he had prayed to see.
The wonder of a Christmas morn
With gifts under the tree.

She was the meaning that he sought
But feared he'd never find.
She was the all-consuming thought
That overwhelmed his mind.

And ev'ry dream he dared to dream
Had been a dream of her.
To him, she had been ev'rything
That caused his heart to stir.

The Show Had Been the Only Thing

The show had been the only thing
In which they had believed,
And they began to wallow in
The plaudits they received.

But in the moment, they forgot
How hard it was at first
With all the toil and energy
And steps that they had cursed.

Although now it's second nature,
Back then it was a chore.
An experience forgotten
Or chosen to ignore.

But now the show was well rehearsed,
And they performed it well.
They'd given their true diligence,
And this was their sequel.

And on the circus, they relied
Where lived their family.
The show had been the only thing
That brought serenity.

Gordon Bostic

What Should He Say?

He pondered what to say to them
As they all stared at him.
What words of wisdom did he have
That were not sad and grim?

It's overcoming obstacles
That makes our lives worthwhile
And dealing with the challenges,
Both easy and the vile.

For life does not point out a path.
It's up to us to find.
And though there may be handicaps,
They're mainly in our mind.

For perseverance does pay off,
And they had proved it's true.
Resiliency, the only word
To mark what they'd been through.

"Accept yourself for who you are,"
Was all he had to say.
"You are unique unto this world
And meant to be that way."

Kris's Thoughts

The circus had been magical
And where they fell in love.
A feeling that was new to her
That she knew nothing of.

As loner, she had always been
With no desire to change.
Until the young man that she met
Had made her feel so strange.

Then when she came to recognize
The feeling had been love.
As though an angel came to her
From somewhere high above.

Whatever outcome there may be
Arising from this strife.
The circus had her gratitude
Because it changed her life.

Gordon Bostic

Burnt Bridges

Kris went to Bryce and asked of him
If there was any way
He could look back to his past life
And try to save the day.

She knew it was a lot to ask,
But these were desp'rate times.
And only he may hold the key
Before the last clock chimes.

But Bryce had said he cut those ties
A long, long time ago.
He was not sure they would respond
Or cared about the show.

His pride he'd have to push away
To proffer a request.
And pray someone found in their heart
A reason to invest.

He begged and pleaded and cajoled
But all to no avail.
For all who were society
Had prayed to see it fail.

Bryce told Kris he had done his best,
But he'd found no success.
He burnt his bridges long ago,
And that could not redress.

Beliefs Can Be Delusional

Beliefs can be delusional
If we believe too hard.
When we ignore the evidence
That we should not discard.

Beliefs are based on rationale
Or reasons that we find.
But sometimes we believe in things
Because of state of mind.

We pray for hope when there is none.
For peace when there is war.
Believing if we pray enough,
We'll get what we pray for.

Beliefs can be delusional
If we too hard believe
To find what we had wished was true
Is not what we receive.

Kris and Bryce

Though Bryce was still recovering,
He wanted to be there
To lend them his encouragement
And watch Kris in the air.

For now, he had been wheelchair bound
But still had life to live.
And found he's even luckier
Since Kris chose to forgive.

His demons he had pushed aside
And clutched reality.
For he had done a hero's job
Despite the penalty.

Whether or not it may be true
With this, their final show,
There was a path laid out for them
Where they both wished to go.

Although their friends they'd sorely miss
It also had been true
That Kris and Bryce had future plans
With things they planned to do.

A Celebration

They ran into the center ring
And applauded the crowd.
For in the tragedy, they found
A reason to be proud.

Although they did not look the part
When it came time to shine
They sacrificed to save the crowd
When lives were on the line.

As many wise men have declared,
It's not about the skin
But rather it's the character
And what may lie within.

If this would be their final show,
They'd like the crowd to see
It had been a celebration
Of all humanity.

Epilogue

Then after the show concluded,
They gathered one last time
Where they spoke about achievements
And how far was the climb.

They spoke about the fun they had,
The sorrow, and the pain.
And if they knew what laid ahead,
They'd do it all again.

They all confirmed how proud the were
This risk they chose to take.
For purpose, they believed they proved
Now left within their wake.

They came together one last time
To celebrate the show.
Then they dispersed into the night
With nowhere else to go.

About the Author

Gordon Bostic was born in West Virginia and grew up in Virginia. A graduate of James Madison University and Fairleigh Dickinson University, he worked as a computer scientist and a software engineer for most of his life. He began writing at a young age as a way of expressing himself, his feelings, and his view of the world. Gordon has also had an interest in telling his stories in one way or another. A Celebration of Humanity is his fifth novel. Gordon currently lives on the Jersey Shore with his wife, Susan

www.ingramcontent.com/pod-product-compliance
Lightning Source LLC
Chambersburg PA
CBHW020413150626
46554CB00013B/854